BLOOMINGTON PUBLIC LIBRARY

P9-CRK-285

15229

101505
O (2003)

BLOOMINGTON PUBLIC LIBRARY

205 E. OLIVE STREET

POST OFFICE BOX 3308

BLOOMINGTON, ILLINOIS 61701

OCT 0 5

DEMCO

EXPLORING THE WORLD

COOK

James Cook Charts the Pacific Ocean

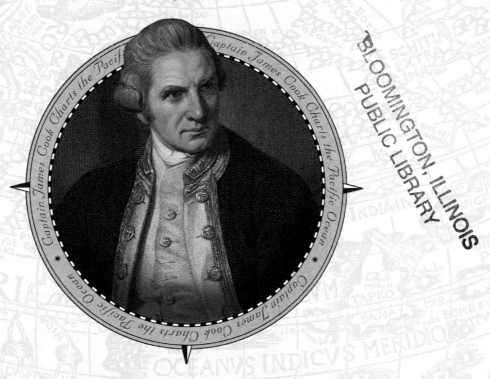

BLOOMINGTON, ILLINOIS PUBLIC LIBRARY

BY JEAN KINNEY WILLIAMS

Content Adviser: Len Travers, Ph.D., Department of History,
University of Massachusetts, Dartmouth, Massachusetts

Reading Adviser: Dr. Linda D. Labbo, Department of Reading Education,
College of Education, The University of Georgia

COMPASS POINT BOOKS
MINNEAPOLIS, MINNESOTA

Compass Point Books
3109 West 50th Street, #115
Minneapolis, MN 55410

Visit Compass Point Books on the Internet at *www.compasspointbooks.com* or
e-mail your request to *custserv@compasspointbooks.com*

Photographs ©: Stock Montage, cover, 1, 15; North Wind Picture Archives, back cover (background), 14, 20, 26, 32; Hulton/Archive by Getty Images, 4, 7, 21, 31, 40; Corbis, 5, 17 (top); Douglas Peebles/Corbis, 8; Kevin Schafer/Corbis, 9; Fine Art Photographic Library/Art Resource, N.Y., 10; Michael S. Yamashita/Corbis, 11; Bettmann/Corbis, 12, 16, 25, 27, 38; Gianni Dagli Orti/Corbis, 17 (bottom); Christel Gerstenberg/Corbis, 18; Macduff Everton/Corbis, 19; PhotoDisc, 22; Daniel Zupanc/Bruce Coleman Inc., 23; Giraudon/Art Resource, N.Y., 24; Ann Hawthorne/Corbis, 28; Digital Stock, 29; Craig Tuttle/Corbis, 33; Robert Garvey/Corbis, 34; Historical Picture Archive/Corbis, 36; Mike Zens/Corbis, 37; SEF/Art Resource, N.Y., 41.

Editors: E. Russell Primm, Emily J. Dolbear, Melissa McDaniel, and Catherine Neitge
Photo Researcher: Svetlana Zhurkina
Photo Selector: Linda S. Koutris
Designer: The Design Lab
Cartographer: XNR Productions, Inc.

Library of Congress Cataloging-in-Publication Data
Williams, Jean Kinney.
  Cook : James Cook charts the Pacific Ocean / by Jean Kinney Williams.
    v. cm. — (Exploring the world)
 Contents: More than a great explorer—Exploring Tahiti—New Zealand, Australia, but no
new continent—A short time at home—Another question about the globe—The last expedition-
and no northwest passage—A sudden and gruesome ending.
  ISBN 0-7565-0421-X (hardcover)
  1. Cook, James, 1728–1779—Juvenile literature. 2. Explorers—Great Britain—Biography—
Juvenile literature. 3. Pacific Ocean—Discovery and exploration—Juvenile literature. [1. Cook,
James, 1728–1779. 2. Explorers. 3. Voyages around the world.] I. Title. II. Series.
  G246.C6 W58 2003
  910'.92—dc21   2002009922

© 2003 by Compass Point Books
All rights reserved. No part of this book may be reproduced without written permission
from the publisher. The publisher takes no responsibility for the use of any of the materials
or methods described in this book, nor for the products thereof.
Printed in the United States of America.

Table of Contents

NOTE: In this book, words that are defined in the glossary
are in **bold** the first time they appear in the text.

More than a Great Explorer

In the 1700s, the American **colonies** were breaking away from Great Britain. Around that same time, English explorer James Cook was looking for new lands to claim for his country.

During his remarkable career, Cook sailed around the world three times. On the first of these trips, he helped to establish the British in Australia. Cook did much more than just discover lands for Great Britian to control, however. He made important contributions to knowledge about geography, which is the study of Earth's people, resources, climate, and physical features. Cook carefully charted and mapped parts of the world that were otherwise unknown to Europeans. These charts and maps remained in

James Cook, explorer for Great Britain

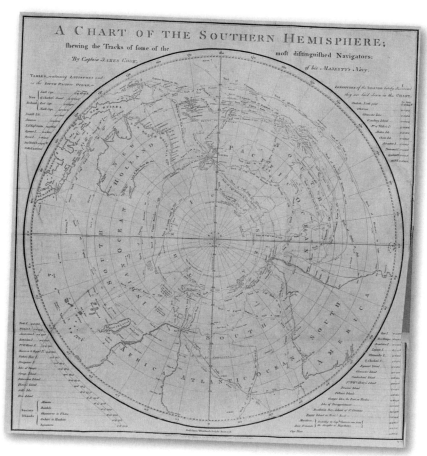

Cook's maps were important to eighteenth century Europe.

use until the 1900s.

James Cook also did much to improve the treatment of sailors. Before Cook, many sailors on long voyages suffered from **scurvy.** This disease result-ed from not getting enough vitamin C. Cook made sure his crew ate well and had clean living quarters. Later, ship captains treated their crews based on Cook's example.

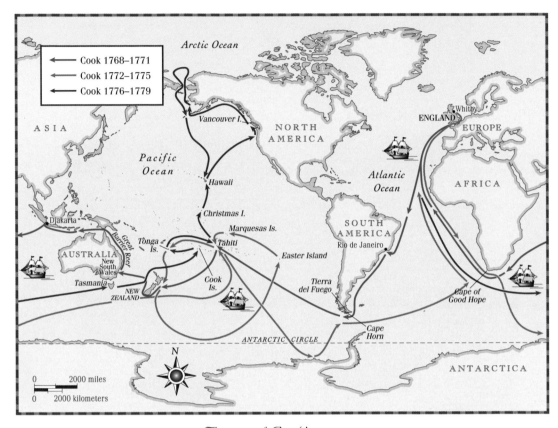

A map of Cook's voyages

England's medical and scientific community rewarded Cook for his success in preventing scurvy. He rose to high ranks in the British navy. He was made a member of the Royal Society. This was a group of well-educated, wealthy Englishmen. The society's goal was to advance the study of science. In Cook's day, almost no one from his poor background moved into the British navy's upper ranks or joined the Royal

Society. Cook, however, was remarkable.

Cook was both courageous and curious. His talents helped Great Britain during the time known as the **Age of Enlightenment.** During this era, new ideas and experiments brought progress to many fields, from science to literature to philosophy. Cook's many contributions to the Age of Enlightenment ensured his place as one of the world's greatest explorers.

Cook had many new thoughts about British exploration, and he recorded some of these in a journal.

A Self-Made Man

James Cook was born on October 27, 1728, in England. He came from a village in Yorkshire called Marton-in-Cleveland. His father managed a farm. It was clear to everyone

Cook's Yorkshire cottage was moved to Fitzroy Gardens in Melbourne, Australia.

Cook learned about ocean navigation at the seaport of Whitby.

that young James was intelligent, so his father's employer helped pay for him to attend school.

As a teenager, James began working for a shopkeeper in a small seaport town. James was more interested in the ocean than in the shop, though. So in 1746, he made his way to a larger seaport called Whitby.

James was hired by brothers named John and Henry Walker, who owned a coal-shipping business.

For the next nine years James Cook learned about sailing as he taught himself **navigation, astronomy,** and mathematics. He sailed in the North Atlantic, which was dangerous because

Cook wanted to become a member of the British navy.

of its violent storms, thick fog, and rocky coasts. Cook was fearless, however. In 1755, the Walkers offered Cook command of his own **collier,** or coal ship. Cook turned them down. He had decided to join the British Royal Navy to enjoy new challenges and see more of the world.

In the navy, Cook's calm manner and experience helped him move quickly up the ranks. Cook served during the French and Indian War (1755–1763), a war between England and France that took place in North America. He became well known when he directed a warship up the difficult Saint Lawrence River to attack the city of Quebec, in what is now Canada. After the war ended in 1763, Cook returned to England and married a woman named Elizabeth Batts.

He spent the next five years

Cook gained fame by navigating the often treacherous Saint Lawrence River during the French and Indian War.

Cook was a popular and intelligent pilot.

mapping the coast of Newfoundland, part of present-day Canada, for the British navy. He returned home to spend the winter months with his family, which over time grew to include six children.

Cook became a highly respected naval officer. Both his **superiors** and the men he commanded admired him. He was a skilled pilot and leader aboard ship. His interest in science made him even more valuable as a ship captain.

In 1769, the Royal Navy planned to send a ship to the recently discovered island of Otaheite—known today as Tahiti—in the South Pacific. Astronomers had predicted that the planet Venus would pass between Earth and the Sun in June of that year. Tahiti was one of three spots on Earth where this could be seen. Secretly, the Royal Navy also wanted to look for a continent that was thought to exist somewhere in the Southern **Hemisphere.** Some scientists believed that a large landmass must exist there to balance all the land in the Northern Hemisphere, which included North America, Africa, Asia, and Europe. The navy decided James Cook was the right captain for the voyage.

Exploring Tahiti

Cook chose a collier called the *Endeavour* to make the journey to Tahiti. From his days in the coal business, Cook knew that colliers were sturdy and roomy, just what was needed for a long trip. A number of scientists traveled with Cook on the trip. One was an astronomer named Charles Green, who would study Venus as it passed in front of the Sun. Another, Joseph Banks, was a **botanist,** or plant expert. Artists also came along to draw any newly discovered plants and animals.

The *Endeavour* set sail from England on August 26, 1768. Cook headed south along the coasts of Europe and Africa, and then west across the Atlantic Ocean to South America. By December, the

Botanist Joseph Banks

The Endeavour

Endeavour had reached the frigid southern tip of South America. After rounding Cape Horn, the ship headed out across the Pacific. Finally, in April 1769, Cook and his crew saw the beautiful beaches of Tahiti in the distance.

The crew arrived healthy. Cook always insisted that the sailors' quarters be clean. He also made sure that they ate better than many sailors of the time. They had the usual daily

Citrus fruit was another source of vitamin C that could prevent sailors from becoming ill with scurvy.

dry biscuits and salted pork. But the men also ate sauerkraut, a dish made from cabbage, because it was rich in vitamin C. The men needed vitamin C to prevent scurvy.

As the *Endeavour* neared Tahiti's Matavai Bay, the island's natives paddled out in canoes to greet the newcomers. When the English landed, they were given a tour of the natives' villages. They also received gifts of food.

The English scientists and artists got busy studying and drawing the lush plants that were new to them. At the same time, Cook and Green prepared to study Venus. In June, they made careful notes as Venus

passed in front of the Sun. While in Tahiti, Cook also mapped the island's entire coastline, and the ship's hull was cleaned. By August, it was time to move on.

Cook made a study of the planet Venus.

Relations between the English and Tahitians had become tense. One problem between the two groups would be common throughout Cook's South Pacific

The Tahitians brought Cook and his crew gifts of food.

Members of Cook's crew were impressed with the Tahitians' tattoos.

travels. The islanders often stole knives, clothing, or other items from the English.

Yet the two groups experienced times of friendship, too. Many of the sailors admired the Tahitians' tattoos. By the time Cook left Tahiti, some of his crew had tattoos of their own. Today, tattoos are still common among sailors.

On to Australia

When Cook's work on Tahiti was done, it was time for him to carry out his secret assignment for the Royal Navy. The British feared that French explorers would find the southern continent and claim it for France. Cook was to find it first and make it Great Britain's. Cook did not believe he would find a large continent, but he followed orders and headed south.

In October 1769, his men sighted present-day New Zealand, two large islands in the Pacific. Cook spent the next six months sailing around

The New Zealand coast that Cook sighted in 1769

the islands, charting the coastline. Shallow, sandy waters made this difficult. Cook and his men sometimes saw the islands' native people, called the Maoris, on the beaches. Some Maoris used their warlike dances to show the English that they were not welcome there.

In December, the *Endeavour* hit a rock and began taking on water. Cook found a cove he named Queen Charlotte's Sound, where the

Tawhaio, king of the Maori people

ship could stop for repairs. The Englishmen met friendlier Maoris while repairing the ship. They learned that bones lying on the beach belonged to the Maoris' enemies. They had been partially eaten. By the end of March 1770, Cook had mapped the entire coastline of New Zealand. It had been almost two years since he had left England, but he was not yet ready to return. He did not know it at the time, but he still had another

James Cook after his landing at Botany Bay

stop to make: Australia.

The *Endeavour* reached Australia's east coast one month later. An exploring party went ashore near present-day Sydney. The area was filled with plants the Europeans had never seen before. Banks, the ship's botanist, was so thrilled at the many new plants that

Cook called their landing spot **Botany** Bay.

The ship continued north along the coast, sailing through an area called the Great Barrier Reef. This is among the most dangerous sailing waters in the world because the reef is made of sharp **coral,** which can tear into a ship. Cook was careful,

The Endeavour *was damaged by a coral spike while sailing through the Great Barrier Reef.*

but a coral spike finally pierced the *Endeavour.* It caused serious damage. A crew member named Jonathan Monkhouse came to the rescue. He recalled an old sailor's trick of wrapping a sail around a hole to bandage it for a short time. This helped the *Endeavour* stay afloat long enough to get to a beach for repair.

It took seven weeks to repair the ship. The crew rested. They also looked on in amazement at an animal they had never seen before. "It was of a mouse colour, very slender and swift of foot," Cook wrote in his journal, but the animal was much larger than a mouse. This unfamiliar animal was the kangaroo. Cook's men also discovered it tasted delicious.

Cook and his crew were amazed at seeing kangaroos for the first time.

In August 1770, Cook continued north along the eastern shore of Australia. He named the territory New South Wales and claimed it for Great Britain. Australia was not the huge continent the Royal Navy had hoped Cook would find; it was time for him to return to England.

On the way home, the *Endeavour* stopped at what is today Djakarta, Indonesia, where many of the sailors became ill. Thirty-three men died, including Jonathan Monkhouse and the astronomer, Charles Green.

The *Endeavour* finally arrived back in England in July 1771. It had been at sea for three years.

A Second Journey

The British people wanted to know everything about the adventures of the *Endeavour.* Cook, however, preferred to spend time with his family. Everyone from naval commanders to King George III praised Cook for all he had accomplished during his journey. They were especially impressed with how he had prevented his sailors from getting scurvy. Cook also brought back new charts showing 5,000 miles (8,047 kilometers) of coastlines in the Pacific, along with important information about New Zealand and Australia.

Even George III was impressed by Cook.

Still, there were huge areas in the Pacific left to explore. Cook was promoted to commander, and another trip was planned.

Cook had command of the Resolution.

This time, Cook would have two colliers, and would approach the Pacific from the opposite direction. The ships would explore south of Africa's Cape of Good Hope and then head to New Zealand. Cook commanded a ship called the *Resolution.* A smaller ship, the *Adventure,* was under the command of Captain Tobias Furneaux. They left England in July 1772.

As Cook's two ships rounded the southern tip of Africa and neared Antarctica, they were tossed by heavy winds. Cook had learned to sail on the frigid North Atlantic, so he was not frightened by the ice that coated everything. By mid-December, his men spotted what appeared to be land. It was actually a huge iceberg. They all knew that crashing into an iceberg would mean the end of their journey— and their lives. Still, Cook continued south. On January 17, 1773, Cook wrote, "We crossed the **Antarctic Circle,** and are undoubtedly the first and only ship that ever crossed that line." Finally, ice made it impossible to go on, so they sailed north.

Over the next few weeks, Cook would turn the ship south to see if there was land ahead, get stopped by ice, and then go northeast before sailing south

Icebergs made Cook's journey in the Antarctic especially difficult.

The Resolution *left the coast of New Zealand before Cook reunited with Furneaux.*

again. In February, the two ships lost each other in fierce winds and fog. The captains had agreed to meet in New Zealand if that happened.

The *Resolution* and the *Adventure* met up in New Zealand in April. Then they headed east and northeast to hunt for unknown land. They traveled halfway to South America without seeing anything before turning back.

Back in New Zealand, bad weather again separated the two ships. The *Adventure* was pushed far out to sea, and the *Resolution* left New Zealand before Furneaux could return. Cook left him a message in a bottle buried in a marked spot on the beach at Queen Charlotte's Sound.

Cook wanted to continue exploring near the Antarctic Circle. In January 1774, the *Resolution* came within 75 miles (121 km) of the coastline of Antarctica. This was the far-thest south that any ship had traveled at that time. After finding—and battling—nothing but ice, Cook concluded that no large continent existed in the Southern Hemisphere north of the Antarctic.

As the *Resolution* made its way back from the Antarctic,

Cook came closer to the coast of Antarctica than any other explorer of his time.

The stone statues of Easter Island

Cook stopped to explore Easter Island. This island had been discovered fifty years earlier, but there was no map of it. Easter Island would later become famous for the huge ancient stone statues that dot the island. Many of the human-like figures, some 40 feet (12 meters) tall, look out to sea. They appear to be guarding the island. "We could not help wondering how they were set up, indeed if the Island was once Inhabited by a race of Giants," Cook wrote.

The *Resolution* made a few more stops before returning to Queen Charlotte's Sound in October 1774. There, Cook discovered that the message in the bottle he had left for Furneaux was gone. Furneaux had found it and left for England. Cook's ship did not return to England until July 1775.

Searching for the Northwest Passage

Cook's second trip was among the most remarkable in the history of sailing. He had covered 70,000 miles (112,654 km) of the vast Pacific Ocean. Yet he had not lost a single sailor to scurvy. This was the first time that a ship commander could say that. It was especially remarkable because it was a three-year journey.

Cook became a member of the Royal Society. The society also awarded him its gold medal. Cook met again with King George and was promoted once more. He also was given an important job at Greenwich Hospital. This gave him the chance to spend time with his family. He had not spent much time at home during the past seven years.

Cook soon found himself frustrated with his hospital job. He wanted to sail again. Another question about Earth still needed an answer: Was there a water route through North America that connected the Atlantic and Pacific oceans? Cook wanted to search for what was called

The Royal Society awarded Cook this medal.

The Discovery

the **Northwest Passage** from the west coast of North America. Other explorers who had searched for the Northwest Passage had started from the east coast. Cook began planning for another major voyage.

Once again, Cook took two ships on his journey. Cook commanded the *Resolution* again. The second ship was called the *Discovery.*

The two ships left England in July 1776. From the start, Cook seemed gloomy and irritable. It did not help that damage to the *Resolution* from the previous voyage had not been properly fixed. Leaking was a constant problem, and the sailors were often forced to do repairs. Still, by February 1777, they had reached New Zealand.

From there, the ships traveled north to the present-day Cook Islands, which were

A lagoon in the Cook Islands

*The appropriately named Christmas Island
was spotted on December 25, 1777.*

named after Captain Cook. Cook made what would be his last visit to Tahiti in August. He gave gifts of horses, cows, and other animals from King George to the Tahitian people before moving on.

On December 25, 1777, Cook's party came across an island they had not known about. They named it Christmas Island. Three weeks later, continuing north in the Pacific, Cook sailed to another group of islands. He named them the Sandwich Islands after his good friend in the British navy, the earl of Sandwich. Today, the Sandwich Islands are called Hawaii.

By March 1778, the ships had crossed the Pacific and reached what is now Oregon. Cook headed north up the coastlines of western Canada and Alaska. He spent seven months searching for **inlets** that might be the Northwest Passage. He never succeeded. Finally, the ships were stopped by the same force they met at the other end of the world: solid ice. Cook decided to leave before the frigid winter arrived. He headed back to Hawaii. In January 1779, his ships settled into Kealakekua Bay on the island of Hawaii.

The first time Cook and his men had arrived in Hawaii was the first time the native people there had ever seen Europeans. They thought

Captain Cook during his journey to Alaska

Cook might be a god. When Cook returned after his trip to Alaska, however, one of his sailors died. Cook's men buried the man on the beach. The Hawaiians knew then that the Europeans were just people like them. From then on, relations between the native Hawaiians and the English became tense. Cook's ships left in February. Soon

*Hawaiian shores would not be a friendly place
for Cook and his crew in 1779.*

Cook's second journey to Hawaii was nothing like his first (shown here). By 1779, the natives no longer respected him.

after, the *Resolution* needed repairs, so Cook and his crew turned back to Hawaii. The Hawaiians were not happy to see them return.

A Sudden End

Cook was not happy to return to Hawaii, either. The Hawaiians sometimes stole from the Europeans. Cook had grown tired of it. When a small boat carried on the *Discovery* was stolen, Cook went ashore. He demanded that a local chief be held hostage until the boat was returned. Hawaiians gathered on the beach. They were armed with clubs, rocks, and knives. They turned on Cook and the sailors with him. Cook and his men were unable to get back to the ships before they were clubbed and stabbed to death.

Sailors on the ships watched the events in horror. They were stunned. From one of the ships came the cry, "We have lost our father!"

Many of the men had been with Cook for all three of his great journeys. They would have traveled anywhere with him. Cook expected hard work from his crew, but he treated them fairly and did all he could to bring them home alive. By insisting on cleanliness and a proper diet, Cook made the job of a sailor much safer. Men who traveled with Cook knew they

James Cook died in a dispute with Hawaiians.

had helped him add much to what was known about the world.

Cook's men took his body from the island. They buried the great explorer at sea. Then they began the long trip back to England.

A statue of James Cook in Sydney, Australia

Glossary

Age of Enlightenment—a period of time during the 1700s noted for its scientific discoveries and its new ideas about art and philosophy

Antarctic Circle—an imaginary line near Antarctica; areas south of the Antarctic Circle have at least one day during the winter when the sun never rises

astronomy—the study of planets, stars, and other objects in space

botanist—a scientist who studies plants

botany—the study of plants

collier—a ship that carries coal

colonies—territories settled by people from other countries and controlled by those countries

coral—hard, sharp structures made up of the skeletons of millions of tiny creatures

hemisphere—half of a sphere, especially of Earth

inlets—narrow bodies of water that lead inland from larger bodies of water, such as oceans

navigation—the method of setting the course of a ship

Northwest Passage—a water route once believed to exist across North America connecting the Atlantic and Pacific oceans

scurvy—a deadly disease caused by not getting vitamin C for a long period of time

superiors—people who are higher in rank or position

Did You Know?

❧ During their travels in the Antarctic, James Cook and his crew experimented by bringing aboard blocks of ice from icebergs and melting them into drinking water.

❧ While sailing along the New Zealand coast, Cook and his men named the land formations Duck Cove, Woodhen Cove, and Seal Rocks after the animals they hunted for food in that area.

❧ German scientist Johann Reinhold Forster sailed with Cook to Antarctica and became the discoverer of the emperor penguin. He was the first natural scientist to make it to Antarctica.

❧ The British Royal Navy had such a hard time finding sailors for its ships that it sometimes forced criminals to join.

❧ The Maori natives of New Zealand had "battleships" of their own—large canoes that could hold as many as one hundred warriors.

❧ When Hawaiian natives battled with Cook and his crew in 1779, the natives' tightly-woven shields were actually bullet-proof.

❧ Elizabeth Batts Cook outlived her husband James and all six of their children. The Cooks' two eldest sons, James and Nathaniel, both died at sea.

Important Dates in Cook's Life

1728
James Cook
born in
Yorkshire,
England

1768
Cook leaves for
Tahiti and hopes
to find another
continent in the
Pacific

1770
The
Endeavour
lands in
Botany Bay,
Australia

1775
Cook is made a
member of the
Royal Society

1779
The Resolution
makes two trips
to Hawaii; during
the second, Cook
is killed during a
conflict with
the natives

1769
Cook and the
crew of the
Endeavour arrive
in Tahiti and also
explore the New
Zealand coast

1755
Cook joins
England's Royal
Navy and goes
on to serve in
the French and
Indian War

1772–1775
Cook commands the
Resolution, one of two
English ships used for
further exploration of the
Pacific; the crew crosses
the Antarctic Circle and
visits Easter Island

1776–1778
Cook sets out for a
second time with the
Resolution; instead of
finding the Northwest
Passage, he revisits
Tahiti, explores various
islands in the South
Pacific, and travels
along the Alaskan
and Canadian coasts

Important People

JOSEPH BANKS (1743–1820) botanist who traveled on the *Endeavour* and brought back information about the new plants and animals discovered during the journey

TOBIAS FURNEAUX (1735–1781) captain who commanded the *Adventure* during Cook's 1772 voyage

KING GEORGE III (1738–1820) English king at the time Cook made his voyages

CHARLES GREEN (1735–1771) astronomer who sailed with Cook aboard the *Endeavour*

JONATHAN MONKHOUSE (?–1771) sailor who successfully bandaged the *Endeavour* when it sprung a leak after scraping a piece of coral

JOHN (?) AND HENRY WALKER (?) brothers who owned the coal-shipping business to which Cook was apprenticed in 1746

Want to Know More?

At the Library

Bowen, Richard. *Captain James Cook*. Broomall, Pa.: Mason Crest
    Publishers, 2002.

Brodenek, Enid. *James Cook*. Milwaukee: Gareth Stevens, 2001.

Gaines, Ann Graham. *Captain Cook Explores the Pacific in World History*.
    Springfield, N.J.: Enslow, 2002.

Hesse, Karen. *Stowaway*. New York: Simon & Schuster, 2000.

Meltzer, Milton. *Captain James Cook: Three Times around the World*.
    Tarrytown, N.Y.: Marshall Cavendish, 2001.

On the Web

For more information on *James Cook*, use FactHound
to track down Web sites related to this book.

1. Go to *www.facthound.com*
2. Type in a search word related to this
   book or this book ID: 075650421X
3. Click on the *Fetch It* button.

Your trusty FactHound will fetch the best Web sites for you!

Through the Mail

Captain Cook Memorial Museum
Grape Lane
Whitby, North Yorkshire YO22 4BE
England
Allows visitors to explore the house where
Cook served his apprenticeship and to see
several artifacts from his voyage

On the Road

The Mariners' Museum
100 Museum Drive
Newport News, VA 23606
757/596-2222
800/581-7245
To learn about the Age of Exploration and
view exhibits of ships and maritime artifacts

Index

About the Author

Jean Kinney Williams lives and writes in Cincinnati, Ohio. Her nonfiction books for children include *Matthew Henson: Polar Adventurer* and a series of books about American religions. She is also the author of *The Pony Express, African-Americans in the Colonies,* and *Ulysses S. Grant.*